AIR AND FLYING

Barbara Taylor

Photographs by Peter Millard

FRANKLIN WATTS
New York • London • Toronto • Sydney

Design: Janet Watson

Science consultant: Dr. Bryson Gore

Primary science adviser: Lillian Wright

Series editor: Debbie Fox

The author and publisher would like to thank the following children for their participation in the photography of this book: Shaniah Bart, Robin Budhathoki, Mustafa Dungarwalla, Kashif Kazmi, Preya Patel, Donovan Rose, Esha Saha, Timothy Springer, Ruth Staton and Shelley Swann.

Thanks to Carol Olivier of Kenmont Primary School, and Micki Swann.

Illustrations: Linda Costello

Franklin Watts, Inc.
387 Park Avenue South
New York, NY 10016

Library of Congress Cataloging-in-Publication Data
Taylor, Barbara, 1954–
Air and flying / Barbara Taylor.
    p.   cm. – (Science starters)
Includes index.
Summary: Describes the nature and capabilities of air and how it makes flight possible.
ISBN 0-531-14183-7
1. Flight – Juvenile literature. 2. Air – Juvenile literature.
[1. Air. 2. Flight.] I. Title. II. Series.
TL547.T34   1991
629.13 – dc20   90-46261
                                                 CIP   AC

Printed in Belgium

CONTENTS

This book is all about the importance of air to all living things and how animals and machines glide and fly through the air. It is divided into six sections. Each has a different colored triangle at the corner of the page. Use these triangles to help you find the different sections.

These red triangles at the corner of the tinted panels show you where a step-by-step investigation starts.

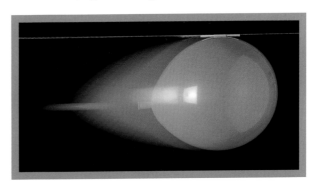

USING AIR

How does an airplane take off and stay up in the air?

An airplane is much heavier than air. But it is lifted upward by air moving past its wings. The shape of the wings helps an airplane to take off and stay up in the air (see pages 19-21). Once an airplane is in the air, the power of its engines pushes it along. As long as air keeps moving quickly past the wings, the plane will not fall down to the ground.

Our planet Earth is wrapped in a blanket of air called the atmosphere. Out in space, there is no air, but on Earth air is everywhere. It is inside your body and fills the spaces all around you. When a mug or a bowl looks empty, it is really full of air. You can't see, smell or taste air but you can see the effect it has on other things. Bubbles of air are whisked into some foods, such as mousses or meringues, to make them light and fluffy.

One useful thing about air is that it can be squashed or compressed into a smaller space. By blowing very hard, this boy can compress a lot of air inside this plastic parrot. We use compressed air inside bicycle tires. The air works like a cushion to keep us from feeling all the bumps in the road. Compressed air can be very powerful. It is used to drive drills that can dig right through surfaces as hard as concrete or ashphalt.

AIR FOR LIFE

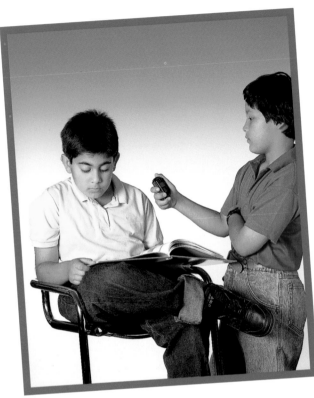

How many times do you breathe in one minute? Use a watch or a stopwatch to count the number of breaths you take when you are sitting down relaxing. Do the same thing after one minute of exercise, such as skipping, running in place or cycling. Are the results of each test different? How? You could try out these tests on your friends and compare the results on a chart.

When you breathe in, air goes down a tube into your lungs. Inside your lungs, one of the gases in the air, oxygen, passes into the blood. The blood carries oxygen all around the body. You need oxygen to release the energy from the food you eat. Without oxygen, you would have no energy for all the body processes that keep you alive. Other animals and plants also need oxygen to survive. Oxygen makes up about 20 percent of the air. The rest of the air is mainly another gas called nitrogen (see page 30).

If you put a handful of soil into some water, you should see bubbles of air escaping into the water. The water pushes the air out of the soil and, because air is "lighter," or less dense than water, it rises to the surface. Sandy soil is made of larger particles than clay soil, which means there are larger air spaces between the particles. Compare different soils to find out how much air is trapped between the particles.

Plants and many animals, such as earthworms, live in the soil and feed on the nutrients in it. The roots of plants and the tunnels of earthworms make spaces for air to collect in the soil.

AIR IN WATER

Water contains air, too. The air is dissolved, or spread, through the water in the same way that salt or sugar dissolves in water. Fish and some other animals that live in water get the oxygen they need from air dissolved in water. A fish has special structures called gills to take oxygen out of the water. The gills don't work in air and a fish will suffocate out of the water.

Gills

Gill cover

Some water animals, such as dolphins, cannot take air out of the water. They have to come to the surface to breathe. A dolphin breathes through a special hole, called a blowhole, on the top of its head. Can you see the bubbles of air coming out of this dolphin's blowhole? When underwater, the blowhole is tightly closed so that water cannot get in.

Most people can stay underwater for only a few seconds before they have to come up for air. But by using a snorkel, people can swim near the surface with their head under the water for a long time. They breathe air from above the water through a tube in their mouth.

FLOATING ON AIR

This boy is holding balloons filled with helium. This is a gas that is "lighter," or less dense, than air. The girl has balloons filled with compressed air, which is "heavier," or more dense, than ordinary air. So her balloons are sinking to the ground. Balloons filled with helium are used to carry scientific instruments high into the air to measure the weather.

The different sizes of these three balloons are caused by the temperature of the air inside them. The balloon on the left was kept in a hot place, the one in the middle at room temperature and the one on the right in a cold place.

When air is heated, it spreads out and takes up more space. This makes it less dense than cold air. Cold air takes up less space than hot air, so it is more dense.

Hot-air balloons take
off because the warm
air inside them is less
dense than the air
around them. They
rise up from the
ground and float until
the air inside them
cools down.

The first hot-air balloons were filled with hot air from a small fire lit underneath the balloon. The air inside this balloon was heated with a gas flame. Never try this yourself. Real hot-air balloons today are heated with gas burners. The height of the balloon is controlled by a gas burner carried under the balloon and by throwing extra weight, or ballast, overboard. Unfortunately, there is no way of steering a hot-air balloon. The speed and flight path of the balloon depend on the wind.

AIR RESISTANCE

When anything moves through air, it is slowed down by the force of the air pushing against it. This effect is called resistance, or drag. It acts in the opposite direction to the movement. The way air resistance slows things down can sometimes be useful.

To glide from tree to tree, a flying squirrel spreads out flaps of skin along the sides of its body. The force of gravity pulls the squirrel down to the ground, but the air pushes up against the skin flaps. The high air resistance makes the squirrel fall more slowly.

A ski-jumper glides through the air in a similar way. The resistance of the air pushing against the skis slows down the speed at which the skier falls to the ground.

Parachutes help people to float down safely to the ground from a great height. Air is trapped under the parachute and pushes upward, making the parachute fall slowly.

Investigate parachutes by making some yourself.

1 Cut some squares out of materials, such as paper, cloth and plastic.

2 Tape short pieces of string or thread to each corner.

3 Tie a load, such as a toy, to the strings.

4 Drop the parachutes one at a time from a height and time how long they take to fall to the ground. How does the weight of the load affect the speed at which the parachute falls?

5 Modern parachutes have holes in the canopy so that the air can escape more smoothly. This helps to keep them from wobbling and swaying in the air. Make a hole in the top of your parachutes. How does this change the way they fall to the ground?

Try making a paper helicopter that spins around and around as it falls to the ground.

1 On a piece of paper, draw a shape to match the picture.

2 Cut down the center line and fold along the dotted line so that one rotor bends forward and the other rotor bends backward.

3 Attach a paper clip to the other end of the paper.

4 Drop the helicopter from a height and watch how it spins. Does it turn in the same direction each time you drop it? Bend one of the rotors back in the opposite direction and see what happens. If you drop your helicopter upside down, does it land the right way up? If you cut off one rotor, how does this change the way the helicopter spins?

As the paper helicopter falls, air is trapped underneath the rotors. This pushes the rotors around and makes the helicopter spin. The spinning keeps the helicopter upright and stops it from toppling over as it falls.

Try dropping a flat sheet of paper and a scrunched up sheet of paper from a height. The flat paper will fall more slowly because the air resistance is greater. The amount of air resistance is affected by the shape of an object and the type of surface it has.

Try making some paper gliders like the ones on these two pages (see page 29).

To launch your gliders, hold them level with your ear and throw them as hard as you can. The force of your throw pushes the glider through the air.

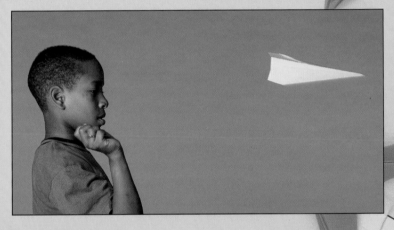

Air pushes up against the flat surfaces of the gliders and stops them from falling too fast. But the amount of air resistance increases as the speed of an object increases. The gliders will fly faster if they have a streamlined shape as this cuts down some of the air resistance and helps air to move past them more easily.

MOVING AIR

The shape of a frisbee helps it to fly further than a paper glider. This special shape is a kind of wing called an airfoil. It is designed to lift the frisbee as it moves through the air. At the same time, it causes very little air resistance so the frisbee can move quickly through the air.

A frisbee has no power of its own to push it through the air. The force needed to make it move comes from the muscles in your arm.

A hang-glider has no pushing power either. It rises upward on warm air currents moving up from the ground. The wings of a hang-glider are shaped like airfoils to lift the glider up into the sky.

To help you understand how airfoils work, you need to investigate how air moves over things and the forces caused by the pressure of this moving air.

Tuck a thin strip of paper into a book and blow over the top of the paper. The paper will lift up into the air. This happens because the air moving quickly over the top of the paper is at a lower pressure than the still air below the paper. The higher pressure of the air below the paper pushes it upward.

Now try blowing between two flags. You may be surprised to see that the flags move closer together instead of blowing apart. The fast-moving air you blow between the flags is at a lower pressure than the still air outside. The higher pressure of the air outside the flags pushes them together.

WINGS

The wing of an airplane is curved on top and almost flat underneath. This is a typical airfoil shape.

Look carefully at the picture. Can you see that the rotors of the helicopter are long, thin airfoils?

The shape of an airfoil means that air moves at different speeds above and below it.

Make a model of an airfoil.

1 Cut out a piece of paper about 1½ in wide and 10 in long.

2 Cut a piece of straw 4 in long.

3 Fold the paper in half and bend one side to make a curved shape. Stick down the edge with tape.

4 Make two holes through the middle of the airfoil and push the straw through the holes. Secure the straw in position with tape.

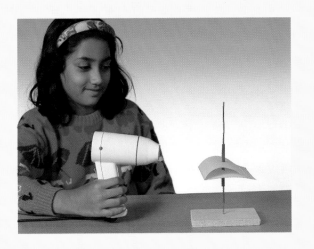

5 Push a long piece of wire through the straw and arrange the airfoil so that it is in a horizontal position.

6 Using a hair dryer, blow air over the airfoil. When the angle of the air is just right, the airfoil should rise up the wire.

The air moves faster over the top of the airfoil than underneath it. This creates low air pressure above the wing and high air pressure beneath it. The airfoil is pushed up by the high air pressure underneath it. This upward pushing force is called lift. It helps airplanes and helicopters to rise into the air.

Low pressure

⬆ ⬆ ⬆ High pressure

POWER FOR FLYING

For air pressure to lift a heavy airplane off the ground, the air has to move past its wings very quickly. The energy to move airplanes through the air comes from a propeller or an engine.

To find out how jet engines work, make a balloon rocket.

1 Cut a straw in half and push one end of a piece of thread or string through the straw.

2 Tie the thread tightly to make a straight line.

3 Blow up a balloon and hold the end firmly so the air cannot escape. Ask a friend to tape the balloon to the straw.

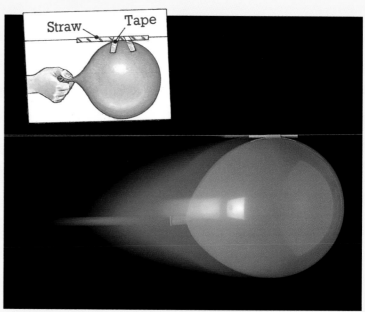

Straw   Tape

4 Pull the balloon to one end of the thread or string and let go. How fast does it move?

The air inside the balloon is at a high pressure because it is compressed into a small space. As air rushes out of one end of the balloon, it pushes the balloon in the opposite direction. An action in one direction causes an equal reaction in the opposite direction.

In a similar way, hot gases rush out of the back of a jet engine and push an airplane forward. Jet engines are very powerful. As they move the airplane forward, the air moving past the wings lifts the plane into the air. Once the plane is in the air, the engines help to overcome the air resistance and keep the plane moving.

A space shuttle is pushed up through Earth's atmosphere by hot gases escaping from the back of the shuttle. The gases are produced by burning solid or liquid fuels. Out in space, where there is no air, the shuttle is not held back by air resistance. It does not need to be pushed through the air by engines as long as it travels in the same direction. But if the shuttle needs to change direction, rocket motors are used.

When the shuttle comes back to Earth, it turns into a very large glider. Can you see that its wings are shaped like airfoils? The shuttle glides back to Earth without any engine power to push it along.

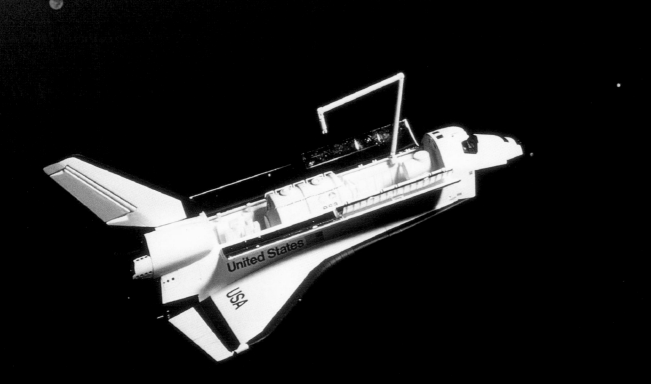

FLYING ANIMALS

Insects, birds and bats are the only animals on Earth that can fly. Instead of engines, their flight is powered by muscles inside their bodies. Insect wings are much thinner and flatter than birds' wings. But as soon as they start flapping and air flows around them, they change shape and become more curved – like airfoils. As an insect flaps its wings down, they push against the air. This pushing moves the insect upward and forward.

The first flying insects on Earth had two pairs of wings, which moved independently in flight. Locusts still fly like this today. But most modern insects with two pairs of wings join the front and back wings together. This makes a bigger surface to push against the air. The wings of bees are linked by little hooks.

Insect flight muscles have to be warm before they will work properly. In cold weather, insects shiver to warm up before take-off. The furry coat of a bee also helps to keep it warm and ready for flight.

Birds are very efficient fliers. They have a smooth, streamlined shape, their front arms are shaped like airfoils, and they have powerful chest muscles to flap their wings up and down. The tail is used for steering.

A bird's wing is a very complicated structure as it can change shape in a huge variety of ways. As the wings beat down, they push the air backward. This makes the bird move forward. When the wings are pulled up again, the tips of the wing feathers move apart to let air flow through. This means the bird has to use less energy pushing against the air.

AIRPLANES

Have you ever built a model airplane? If you look closely at the model, you will find examples of many of the things that help airplanes to take off and fly through the air.

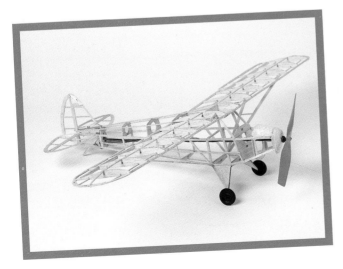

In this model, the energy to drive the propeller comes from a twisted elastic band. As the band unwinds, the propeller turns around.

The wings of the airplane are airfoils – they are curved on top and flatter underneath. This makes the air move faster over the top than underneath and lifts the airplane upward.

A tail flap called a rudder is also used to make the airplane change direction.

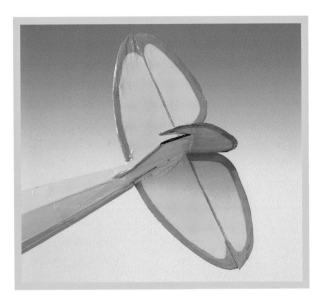

The propeller turns around to pull itself and the plane through the air. It is rather like a wood screw which pulls itself into wood when it is turned.

Flaps on the wings, called ailerons, can be moved to make the airplane turn, climb or dive through the air. The air pressing against the flaps pushes the airplane and makes it change direction.

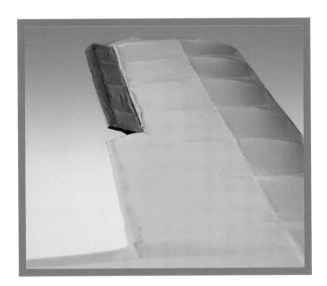

MORE THINGS TO DO

Air in your lungs

Try this investigation to find out more about the air in your lungs. You will need a large plastic bottle, that holds about 4 pints of water, a bowl, some plastic tubing and a waterproof marker pen.

Use a measuring cup to fill the bottle with 1 pint of water and mark the water level on the side of the bottle. Do the same thing with 2 pints, 3 pints and 4 pints of water. Fill the bowl about one third full of water and fill the plastic bottle with water. Hold the bottle over the bowl and put your hand over the top of the bottle. Carefully turn the bottle upside down so that the neck is under the surface of the water. Ask a friend to hold the bottle still for you. Slide the plastic tubing under the neck of the bottle. Adjust the water level in the bottle until it reaches the 4 pint mark. Breathe normally down the tube for one minute and see how the water level changes.

The difference between the two water levels tells you how much air you have blown out of your lungs. Can you figure out how much air you breathe out of your lungs in one hour or one day?

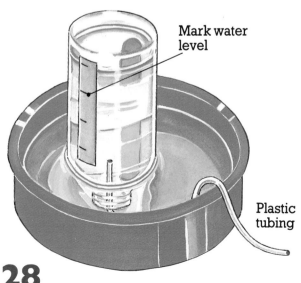

Mark water level

Plastic tubing

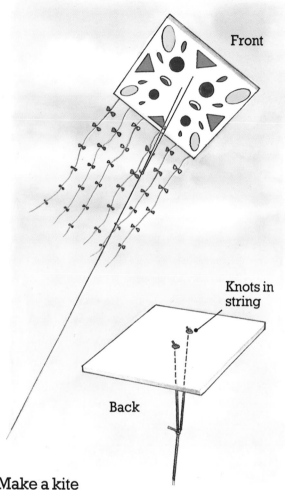

Front

Knots in string

Back

Make a kite

Find the center of a large polystyrene sheet by drawing a line from each corner to the opposite corner. The point where the lines cross is the center. Make one hole through the center and another one 5 in above this point. Thread a loop of string through the holes and tie knots to keep the string from pulling out of the holes. Tie a very long piece of string to the loop. Decorate your kite with colored markers or shiny paper and stick some streamers of paper, yarn or ribbon to one side. On a windy day, take your kite outside and watch the air push it up into the sky.

Making paper gliders

There are lots of different ways of making paper gliders. Here is one way:

1 Take a piece of paper about 12 in by 8 in, fold it in half and open it out again.

2 Fold two of the corners over so they meet in the middle.

3 Fold the same corners to the middle again.

4 Turn the paper over and fold both sides to the middle.

5 Fold the whole glider in half.

6 Grip the glider firmly by the center fold and pull the wings out flat. See how far your glider will fly.

7 Try putting a paper clip or some modeling clay on the nose. How does this change the way the glider flies?

8 Cut some small flaps in the end of the wings. Bend the flaps up and down and see how this changes the direction the glider is flying.

9 Can you design some different shapes for gliders? The pictures on pages 16 and 17 may give you some ideas.

Holes in lid

Make a wormery

Fill a large jar with layers of soil, sand and chalk and add a few earthworms. Put some dead leaves or grass cuttings on top of the soil for the earthworms to eat, and water the soil. Cover the top of the jar with plastic wrap or the lid of the jar. Make holes in the plastic or the lid so the earthworms can breathe. Cover the sides of the jar with black paper – earthworms like the dark. Put the jar in a cool place and keep it damp but not wet. Look at the jar every day and write down what you can see. What happens to the leaves or grass? Can you see any worm casts on the surface of the soil? Are there any burrows in the soil? Do the earthworms mix up the different layers?

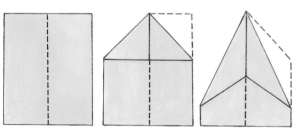

1   2   3

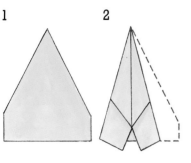

Tape

4   5   6

DID YOU KNOW ?

▲ Air is made up of a mixture of different gases – about 80% nitrogen, 20% oxygen, 0.05% carbon dioxide, 1% inert gases (such as helium, neon and argon). Neon is used in advertising signs and argon in electric light bulbs. The air also contains water vapor, dust particles and pollutants that people have put into the air.

▲ The earliest evidence we have found of flying animals is fossil dragonflies, which flew nearly 300 million years ago. About 200 million years ago, winged reptiles called pterosaurs flew in the skies above the dinosaurs. The first people to leave the ground and fly in the air lived just over 200 years ago, in 1783. They used a hot-air balloon and flew for over five miles.

▲ On December 17, 1903, Orville and Wilbur Wright made the first flights in an aircraft that was heavier than air and could be fully controlled. Their airplane reached a speed of about 30 miles per hour, climbed only a few feet into the air and stayed there for only a few seconds, traveling about 120 feet.

▲ On June 12, 1979, Bryan Allen made the first man-powered flight by pedaling his airplane for three hours across the English Channel. His airplane, the Gossamer Albatross, weighed only 55 pounds and had a wingspan of 96 feet.

▲ Flying fish glide over the surface of the water holding out their huge front fins like wings. They can glide for about 550 yards at a time.

▲ Some flies beat their wings as fast as 1,000 times a second. Some hummingbirds beat their wings at more than 50 beats a second. Hummingbirds can fly sideways, backward and even upside down. A very large bird, such as a swan, beats its wings only one and a half times a second.

▲ A bat's wing is made up of skin stretched over its arm and finger bones. When a bat is flying, its heart beats at 1,000 beats per minute.

▲ In an ancient Greek legend dating back to about 1000BC, Daedalus and his son Icarus made wings of feathers so that they could escape from the island of Crete. The wings were fastened to their shoulders with wax. Icarus flew too near to the Sun so the wax melted and he fell to his death in the sea.

▲ A Boeing 747 "jumbo jet" fully loaded with fuel and 500 passengers weighs more than 350 tons. Yet air pressure underneath the wings lifts it up into the air. The airplane has to reach a speed of about 180 miles per hour before it can take off.

▲ Flying frogs can glide up to 40 feet between trees in the rainforests of southeast Asia. They spread out their large webbed feet, which act like four parachutes to slow down their fall through the trees. They can change direction by moving their legs and changing the shape of their webbed feet.

▲ The space shuttle touches down at a speed of 217 miles per hour – twice as fast as an ordinary airliner.

GLOSSARY

Airfoil
A wing which is curved on top and flat underneath.

Ailerons
Flaps on the wings of an airplane which are moved up or down to make the airplane turn left or right.

Air pressure
The effect caused by the weight of all the air in the atmosphere pressing down on everything.

Air resistance, or drag
The force of the air pushing against things and causing them to slow down or stop.

Atmosphere
The thin layer of air which surrounds Earth and is held there by the pull of Earth's gravity. It is made up of various gases, mainly nitrogen and oxygen.

Compressed air
Air that has been squeezed into a small space.

Density
The mass ("weight") of a substance per unit of volume.

Dissolve
When a solid or a gas mixes completely with a liquid and disappears into it.

Elevators
Flaps on the tail of an airplane which are moved to make the airplane climb or dive through the air.

Gills
The breathing organs of some animals that live underwater. Oxygen passes through the gills into the blood and carbon dioxide passes out of the gills.

Gravity
The force of attraction between any two objects that have mass. The pull of Earth's gravity is very strong.

Helium
A gas that is "lighter," or less dense, than air.

Lift
The force of air pressing up against things which keeps them up in the air.

Lungs
In humans, two large, spongy bags in the chest on either side of the heart. Inside the lungs, oxygen is taken into the blood and carbon dioxide is taken out.

Oxygen
A gas with no taste, color or smell, which is part of air and water. All plants and animals need oxygen to stay alive.

Rotors
The long, thin "wings" of helicopters and autogiros which spin around and around.

Rudder
A flap on the tail of an airplane or the back of a boat which is used for steering.

Streamlined
Something that has a smooth, slim shape, which cuts through air or water easily.

Temperature
A measure of the hotness or coldness of things.

INDEX

Additional photographs:
Allsport/David Cannon 13 (b);
Austin J Brown/APL 4; Bruce
Coleman 24 (t), 25; Stephen
Dalton/NHPA 24 (b); Richard Alan
Wood, Animals Animals/OSF 13
(t); ZEFA 11, 18 (b), 23.
Picture Researcher:
Ambreen Husain

PRINTED IN BELGIUM BY
proost
INTERNATIONAL BOOK PRODUCTION